COSMOLOGY
Exploring the Universe

PETER JEDICKE

A+

PHOTO CREDITS

Page 2: courtesy of NASA, H. Ford (JHU), G. Illingworth (USCS/LO), M.Clampin (STScI), G. Hartig (STScI), the ACS Science Team, and ESA Page 4: courtesy, the Hubble Heritage Team (AURA/STScI/NASA); Pages 5, 12, 13, 16-17,28-29, 35: courtesy, NASA; Pages 8, 20: courtesy Ernest Orlando, Lawrence Berkeley National Laboratory; Page 8: Artwork by Adolf Schaller for STScI. Courtesy NASA and K. Lanzetta (SUNY); Page 9: courtesy Picture History; Page 10: copyright © Lauren Bergholm; Page 14: NASA and H. Richer (University of British Columbia) and NOAO/AURA/NSF; Page15: courtesy Library of Congress; Page 16-17: courtesy NASA, A. Fruchter and the ERO Team, STScI, ST-ECF; Page 19: copyright © Kim Poor; Page 21: Lucent Technologies/Bell Labs; Pages 22, 24, 26, 30: courtesy NASA/WMAP Science Team; Page 25: courtesy NASA/ WMAP Science Team and DMR, COBE, NASA Two-Year Sky Map; Page 27: courtesy NASA Goddard; Page 32: courtesy NASA/Two Micron All-Sky Survey; Page 33: courtesy Todd Boroson/NAOA/AURA/NSF; Page 34: courtesy NASA, C. Palma, S. Zonak, S. Hunsberger, J.Charlton, S. Gallagher, P. Durrell (Pennsylvania State University) and J. English (University of Manitoba); Page 35: courtesy NASA, H. Fort (JHU), G. Illingworth (USCS/LO), M. Clampin (STScI), G. Hartig (STScI), the ACS Science Team, and ESA; Pages 36, 39, 42-43: courtesy Richard Powell; Page 40: copyright © 2003 Pat Rawlings; Page 45: Kevin Hare, Symbolic Computation Group, University of Waterloo.

Published by Smart Apple Media
1980 Lookout Drive, North Mankato, Minnesota, 56003

Produced by Byron Preiss Visual Publications, Inc.
Printed in the United States of America

Copyright © 2003 Byron Preiss Visual Publications

Edited by Howard Zimmerman
Associate editor: Janine Rosado
Design templates by Tom Draper Studio
Cover and interior layouts by Gilda Hannah
Cover art: Courtesy NASA, H. Ford (JHU), G. Illingworth (USCS/LO),
          M. Clampin (STScI), G. Hartig (STScI), the ACS Science Team,
          and ESA

Library of Congress Cataloging-in-Publication Data

Jedicke, Peter.
Cosmology: exploring the universe / by Peter Jedicke.
p. cm. — (Hot Science)
Summary: A discussion of what contemporary science believes regarding the origins and destiny of the universe, as well as what various peoples have believed throughout history.
ISBN 1-58340-366-3

1. Cosmology—Juvenile literature. [1. Cosmology. 2. Universe.] I. Title. II. Series.
QB983.J43 2003   523.1—dc21   2003041649

First Edition

9 8 7 6 5 4 3 2 1

CONTENTS

INTRODUCTION	**Where Did Everything Come From?**	4
CHAPTER 1	**How Everything Began**	7
CHAPTER 2	**The Universe Is This Old**	11
CHAPTER 3	**The Big Bang**	15
CHAPTER 4	**The Young Universe**	20
CHAPTER 5	**The Birth of Galaxies**	24
CHAPTER 6	**The Mystery of What We Can't See**	31
CHAPTER 7	**Where Are the Galaxies Going?**	36
CHAPTER 8	**The Universe as a Ball of String?**	41
GLOSSARY		46
INDEX		47

Where Did Everything Come From?

INTRODUCTION

**Spiral galaxy NGC 4414 is
quite similar in size and shape**

A car comes from a factory, milk comes from a cow, and success comes from trying hard. But all of these things—people, our everyday concerns, and the common things around us—are just a small part of the Big Everything: The Universe. The Universe includes our houses and cities, the whole Earth, all the planets and galaxies, and everything in between. How did it all start? How did we get from the beginning to where we are now? Where will everything end up eventually? Some scientists have even dared to ask whether it happened more than once. These questions belong to the science of cosmology.

To study cosmology, scientists need to understand how things work far beyond our everyday lives. Telescopes, some on mountaintops and some in outer space, give astronomers information about the largest and oldest objects in the Universe, such as galaxies and quasars. Particle accelerators and huge detectors underground tell physicists what the smallest and hottest bits of matter are like.

The Universe is estimated to be about 10^{21} miles (10^{24} km) across. That's a 1 followed by 21 zeroes. Because a billion is worth nine zeroes, a scientist says that the diameter of the Universe is a thousand billion billion miles. Nobody can

The Cone Nebula. This dense region of hydrogen and dust clouds is a stellar nursery. New stars are constantly forming within the nebula, which gives it that wonderful reddish glow.

picture a thousand billion billion miles, so it's important for a cosmology student to be able to do arithmetic with scientific notation.

Cosmology: Exploring the Universe travels all the way out to the farthest edge of the Universe and also back in time to the Universe's birthday. In scientific notation, this happened about 14×10^9 years ago, which means the Universe is about 14 billion years old. It's an arduous trip, and it begins with the history of human curiosity.

Scientific Notation

Cosmological calculations involve numbers so large and so small that the only sensible way to write them down is with scientific notation. Scientific notation is based on the decimal number system and powers of 10. A power of 10 means the number 10 multiplied by itself so many times. The tiny number written in superscript is called the exponent. The exponent tells how many times 10 must be multiplied by itself.

For example:

$10^3 = 10 \times 10 \times 10 = 1,000$ and

$10^6 = 10 \times 10 \times 10 \times 10 \times 10 \times 10 = 1,000,000$

Some examples of large numbers in scientific notation:

$14,000,000,000 = 14 \times 10^9$

$9,500,000,000,000,000 = 95 \times 10^{14}$

For incredibly small numbers, the exponent is written as a negative number.

Some examples of small numbers in scientific notation:

$0.000001 = 10^{-6} = 1/1,000,000$

$0.000000000000000000000000001 = 10^{-27} =$
$1/1,000,000,000,000,000,000,000,000,000$

How Everything Began

CHAPTER ONE

People are curious as to how galaxies, stars, and planets first appeared. They wonder what the Universe is made of and how it began. Every society has told stories about the beginning of the world. A story about how the Universe came from nothing is called a "creation myth." But until human beings began to study the world scientifically, creation myths were just stories. They were not based on facts or data or measurements.

Western civilization can trace its history back to ancient Greece about 3,000 years ago. The word *cosmology* comes from the ancient Greek words meaning "the rules of the Universe." There were many teachers and writers in Greece back then who were the first people ever to share the idea that there are, indeed, *rules* governing the world that are always true, every single time. For instance, the Sun always rises in the east, snow always melts when it is warmed, and the angles in a triangle always add up to 180 degrees. Scientific rules eventually became known as "laws," even though they are not the laws of any government. Nature itself abides by them.

The ancient Greeks had their own creation myths, too. But by the time of Thales, around 550 B.C.E. (Before the Common Era), these were recognized as cultural stories, not scientific theories. Thales was a philosopher who proposed that everything is made of water, but that water changed form in complicated ways to create the variety of things we have in the world. Other Greek philosophers decided that there must be *four* basic elements—water, fire, earth, and air. They suggested that combinations of these basic elements made up everything we see and know. It was also suggested that a fifth form of matter, called "quintessence," was found only in space, far beyond Earth. Eudoxus, a Greek astronomer,

In 1054, people across the world saw the aftermath of a supernova—a massive star exploding—which is still visible today as the Crab Nebula. In 1987, people across the world saw the explosive aftermath of this star going nova. It is designated as Supernova 1987-A.

created a complex explanation for how the planets and stars moved through the quintessence.

The quintessence was thought to be perfect, eternal, and unchanging. This theory was accepted throughout the Dark Ages period in Europe (600–1,000 C.E.), when scientific progress basically came to a complete stop. In the year 1054, Chinese astronomers recorded that they saw a "guest star" in the night sky. It was a supernova—the explosive end to a giant star's existence. This meant that things could change in the starry heavens after all.

Although the event was not recorded in Europe, it was seen there as well. Then, in 1609, Italian scientist Galileo Galilei turned a new invention called the telescope toward the night sky, and ideas rapidly began to change. Within a few generations, scientists realized that the Sun was the center of our solar system. They discovered that the planets, including Earth, travel in orbits around the Sun, and the shapes of these orbits are ellipses, not perfect circles.

Astronomers began to wonder about certain small fuzzy patches in the sky that they could see with their early telescopes. They called them *nebulae*, the Latin word for "clouds." They were separate from, but similar to, the dim, fuzzy strands of the Milky Way that we see across our night sky. They were known as "island universes" in the 19th century. Today we call them galaxies, and we know them to be distant parts of our Universe, not separate universes. But it wasn't until the 20th century that astronomers were able to prove how far away the galaxies are. The distances are staggering and need to be measured using a long yardstick called the light-year. This is the distance that light travels in a single Earth year: about six trillion miles (9.5×10^{15} km). And galaxies are *millions* of light-years distant from us. Andromeda, our closest galactic neighbor, is two million light-years from the Milky Way.

In the 19th century, there was mounting evidence that Earth itself was far older than anyone had ever imagined. Based on information about the layering of the ground under the sea, and similar layering observed in mountain rocks, geologists suggested Earth was many millions, even hundreds of millions, of years old. Then Lord Kelvin, a British scientist, calculated that the Sun had been shining for at least tens of millions of years. Finally, in 1905, Sir Ernest Rutherford suggested that tiny amounts of radioactive minerals in rocks could be used to estimate the age of Earth. Using this technique, we now know that our planet is approximately 4.5 billion years old. (Rutherford, a brilliant British scientist, was respon-

Lord Kelvin, the British scientist who was first to calculate that the Sun had been shining for tens of millions of years.

sible for deducing and describing the physical structure of the atom in 1911.)

The key observation that led the way toward a modern study of cosmology was first made by astronomer Vesto Slipher at Lowell Observatory in Flagstaff, Arizona. In 1914, he noticed that the galaxies were all moving away from our solar system. This amazing fact was the starting point for the great discovery made by astronomer Edwin Hubble: the entire Universe is expanding.

An illustration of the Aztec creation myth. In it, the mother of creation was Coatlique, the Lady of the Skirt of Snakes. She gave birth to Coyolxanuhqui, goddess of the moon, and also to a group of male offspring who became the stars. Coatlique also gave birth to the god of war, who, with the help of a fire serpent, destroyed his brothers and sisters.

Creation Myths from Around the World

• The Navajo of North America told a story of supernatural beings who rose up through the center of an earlier world and set our Universe in order.

• In Africa, the Dogon people said that a cosmic egg, heavier than the whole world, was brought here from the star Sirius and broke in two. One of those broken pieces became our world.

• It is not surprising that the Hawaiian islanders believed the Universe began with supernatural beings throwing volcanic fire at each other. Also according to Hawaiian mythology, a supernatural shark, Kamohoali'i, taught the first humans how to surf.

• Almost 3,000 years ago, the ancient Greeks believed the Universe sprang up when original Chaos (the void that came before anything else) split into Ouranus, or heaven, and Gaia, or Earth.

The Universe Is This Old

CHAPTER TWO

One of the famous "special effects" in physics is called the "Doppler shift." Someone standing on the sidewalk while a fire truck passes by will notice how the pitch of the siren drops as the vehicle speeds past. This is the Doppler shift. The sound waves pile up in front of the truck as it approaches, making the wavelengths seem shorter. This raises the pitch of the siren. As the fire truck drives away, the sound waves stretch out behind the truck, making the wavelengths seem longer. Shorter waves make a higher-pitched sound, while longer ones make a lower-pitched sound. The same principle applies for train whistles, race car engines, or bells on bicycles.

The Doppler shift also applies to light waves. Because the speed of light is so much faster than the speed of sound, the source of the waves has to move much faster than a truck can for the Doppler shift to be noticeable. Objects out there in the Universe are, indeed, moving fast enough to have their Doppler shift measured. To do this, astronomers use an instrument called a "spectroscope." It spreads out the colors of light into a spectrum, arranged in the same order as the colors of a rainbow. In a spectrum, some distinct parallel lines can be seen scratched among the colors. Usually the lines are dark because they represent colors that are missing from the spectrum.

The movement of a star or galaxy towards or away from us makes the lines shift to a slightly different color. A blue shift means the object is moving towards us, and a red shift means the object is moving away from us. Vesto Slipher found that almost all galaxies showed a red shift. Then Edwin Hubble, an astronomer who was working with the largest telescope in the world at the time, figured out that the greater a galaxy's red shift, the farther away from us it is. This conclusion

After being repaired, the *Hubble Space Telescope* is released by the space shuttle's robotic arm and placed back into Earth orbit.

is called "Hubble's Law." A galaxy about 100 million light-years away is traveling at more than 1,200 miles (2,000 km) per second! When Hubble announced his results in 1929, it caused a sensation in the world of science. This was proof that the entire Universe was, and still is, expanding.

Meanwhile, mathematicians had been working with Albert Einstein's famous theory of relativity. They found a way to calculate what the actual shape of the Universe might be. There were three main possible answers. It could be similar to a flat sheet, or perhaps a closed surface such as the outer surface of an inflated balloon, or perhaps an open surface, such as a horse saddle that stretches out forever. The shapes are difficult to describe because the Universe has three dimensions in space (length, width, and height) plus one time dimension, whereas the surface of a sheet, a balloon, or a saddle has only two of those dimensions (length and width).

Until Hubble's Law was announced, experts had no way of telling which model corresponded most closely to the real Universe. But Hubble's Law could help determine the actual shape of the Universe if exact measurements for the speed and distance of enough galaxies could be made. Was the Universe expanding fast enough to never stop, or was the expansion gradually slowing down? This was one of the most significant questions of the 20th century.

Many astronomers worked on observing the red shift of distant galaxies over the years. Finally, in 2001, astronomer Wendy Freedman and a team of scientists got the best answer yet by using the *Hubble Space Telescope*, which was named in Hubble's honor. Freedman's team spent more than 11 years analyzing data from 31 different galaxies to reach their conclusion: the Universe is like an open surface. The galaxies have been spreading apart since the beginning of time, and they will keep on expanding *forever*. The shape of the Universe is totally determined by the expansion. But this is not like a group of children spreading out over a playground, which stretches out in front of them. There is no "playground" over which the Universe can spread—no empty space into which it can expand.

Instead, space *is* the Universe. The expansion of the Universe means space itself is growing larger. The galaxies are being carried along by the outward expansion. There is also no central starting point from which the expansion of the Universe began.

Cosmology experts also use Hubble's Law to calculate backward. Space itself was smaller in the past, and the Universe was all packed in. Thanks to Freedman's evidence, experts estimate that the expansion of the Universe has been going on for about 13 to 14 billion years—which is now taken to be the approximate age of the Universe.

An artist's interpretation of star formation in the early Universe. Clouds of hydrogen gas and dust compress under their own weight. Gravity and pressure cause the clouds to compact. When dense and hot enough, nuclear reactions begin, and a star is born.

The Oldest Stars in the Universe

The age of the Universe as calculated by cosmologists is consistent with what astronomers have discovered about the age of the oldest observable stars. It would hardly make sense to have stars that were older than the Universe! The oldest stars that we can see are found in globular clusters, which are sphere-shaped groups of thousands of stars. Globular clusters are about 100 light-years across, and a galaxy such as the Milky Way has more than 100 globular clusters floating around it. Astronomers analyze a globular cluster by drawing each star as a point on a graph called a "Hertzprung-Russell diagram." Then the shape of the graph indicates how old the entire globular cluster is. This has been done for dozens of separate globular clusters spread around the Milky Way Galaxy, and the average answer is right around 13 billion years.

A globular cluster near the Milky Way Galaxy contains many white dwarf stars, which are some of the oldest stars in the Universe. A patch of the cluster (top rectangle) is blown up to reveal that most of the stars are white dwarfs.

The Big Bang

CHAPTER THREE

A straight line probably seems pretty easy to draw. But Albert Einstein discovered that a straight line is not as simple as it looks. In the second half of his famous theory of relativity, Einstein calculated that really heavy objects—such as the Sun, for instance—slightly warp space and time around them. When passing by a really heavy object, a straight line doesn't look like a straight line after all. This theory was proved in 1919, when pictures of a star behind the Sun were taken during a total eclipse. The light from the star traveled in a line that was bent a little by the mass of the Sun before reaching telescopes on Earth.

Then came an even more astounding conclusion: the curve of the Universe was *changing*. This was based on the mathematical equations of the theory of relativity, which explained how space and time were expanding. The red shift of light from galaxies, seen by astronomers throughout the 1920s, proved that the Universe really is expanding.

A Belgian astronomer, George Edouard Lemaitre, took the next important step. In 1927, Lemaitre suggested that, if the Universe is expanding, it must have been much smaller in the past. There must have been a moment when the Universe was incredibly small. All four dimensions of space and time, and all the matter and energy in the entire Universe, had been wrapped up in what Lemaitre called the "Primeval Atom." (The word *primeval* means "the very earliest time.") There was no time before the Universe began and no space outside the Universe.

A portrait of Albert Einstein. His theories of relativity gave science a new way to look at and understand the Universe.

A Hubble snapshot of some of the Universe's most distant galaxies shows the effects of gravitational lensing. The streaks and curves of light seen here are actually distant galaxies whose light has been split and curved by galaxies closer to Earth. Einstein predicted this gravitational effect.

The scientific name for the first appearance of the Universe is a "singularity." Lemaitre realized that he had explained the birth of the Universe.

The conditions in the Primeval Atom—the "singularity"—were indeed extreme. All the matter and energy that today are spread over approximately 13 billion light-years of space was crushed inside something far smaller than the tiniest speck any microscope can see. No ordinary molecules or atoms or even atomic nuclei could exist in it. The varieties of chemical elements that make up everything in our world were all smashed together, unrecognizable. There was no difference between matter and energy. The four fundamental forces of nature were blended together, acting as one.

No scientist today has a complete theory that can answer all questions about what was happening in the Primeval Atom. The conditions cannot be simulated in a laboratory. Perhaps this amazing little Universe-in-a-microscopic-ball sat there without changing, without a clock to measure time and without a yardstick to measure space. All it needed was a miniscule, random fluctuation to trigger a fantastic transformation. Somehow, the Primeval Atom began to open up.

Around 1950, physicist George Gamow and his colleagues started working on explaining what happened when the Universe began to expand. But there was spirited debate about this extreme view of the origin of the Universe. British astronomer Fred Hoyle was one of the scientists who did not support Gamow's theory. Hoyle preferred to think of the Universe as always being more or less the same as it looks now. Hoyle gave Gamow's theory what he thought was a silly-sounding name: "the Big Bang." Guess what? No one has come up with a better name for what happened when the Primeval Atom blew, and the name has stuck.

The Four Fundamental Forces of Nature

Gravity: This is the force that attracts masses to each other. It is weakest over very short distances but acts over long distances because mass adds up. It explains orbital motion in outer space, and why apples fall down.

Electromagnetism: This is expressed as the attraction or repulsion of charged particles. It is most effective among atoms; beyond that, the positives and negatives tend to balance out. It explains the functioning of light waves, chemistry, electricity, magnetic fields, and why the size of an atom is spread out around the nucleus.

An artist's concept of globular clusters surrounding parts of the Milky Way.

Weak nuclear force: This is expressed as the attraction of nuclear particles—basically the protons and neutrons that are found in the nuclei of atoms. This force applies among nuclear particles only and does not have a noticeable effect on the human scale. It explains the radioactive breakdown of heavy chemical elements.

Strong nuclear force: This is expressed through the attraction of the most basic subatomic particles, called "quarks," to each other. This force is very powerful inside an atomic nucleus but is not effective over distances longer than 10^{-14} m. It explains nuclear reactions and why the mass of an atom is concentrated in the nucleus.

The Young Universe

CHAPTER FOUR

An artist's concept of the Inflationary Period of expansion of the young Universe. As matter and energy expand, subatomic particles stream out from the center.

The Big Bang itself took place at exactly *zero* time. Scientists are sure that, once it started, everything came blasting out of the Primeval Atom so quickly that everyday notions about how long it takes for something to happen are meaningless. The newborn Universe changed more in the first few seconds than it did in the next billion years—and it hasn't exactly been sitting still since then, either! To think about such ultra-short time periods, we need to use scientific notation and keep in mind not just the number of decimal places but also the comparison of one period of time with another.

At approximately 10^{-43} seconds after the Big Bang, gravity separated from the other three forces, and the time of "Grand Unification" began. Grand Unification is the name of the theory that combines the other three forces, but not gravity. This period lasted until 10^{-35} seconds after the Big Bang. The Universe was about 10^{-32} inches (10^{-33} m) in size and the temperature was 10^{27} degrees, still a billion billion times hotter than the center of the Sun.

Although the expansion of the Big Bang was impressive from the very beginning, Grand Unification was followed by a brief spurt of even faster outward expansion, called the "Inflationary Period." This part of the Big Bang was first explained by scientist Alan Guth around 1981 and perfected by other mathematics experts 10 years later. This stage—the Inflationary Period—lasted only from 10^{-35} seconds to 10^{-33} seconds. If we imagine a Big Bang clock that ticked every 10^{-35} seconds, then for 100 ticks of the clock, the size of the entire Universe more than doubled with every tick.

When the Inflationary Period ended, the Universe was a few miles wide—about the size of a mountain. Inflation slowed because quarks and anti-quarks, two of the basic particles of matter, began to absorb the energy of the expansion. The Universe continued to expand, but at more or less the same pace that is still visible today.

As the fictitious Big Bang clock reached the one full second mark, electrons and their anti-matter twins, called "positrons," became dominant in the young Universe. These were part of the overall balance of matter and anti-matter after the Big Bang. When a single electron of matter and a single positron of anti-mat-

Arno Penzias and Robert Wilson stand in front of their "big ear," a radio telescope that first received and recorded the cosmic background radiation. This background "static" was discovered to be the actual initial radiation from the **Big Bang**.

ter meet, they cancel each other out, disappear, and give off an energy particle called a "photon." The photon zips away from the annihilation scene at the speed of light. Cancellation of electrons and positrons caused a rapid increase in the number of photons in the Universe.

Photons, however, can easily be blocked by anything that is not transparent. An opaque object absorbs the energy of the photons it blocks. After the Inflationary Period, the matter in the Universe was, indeed, opaque. The absorbed energy from the photons kept the matter hot, and it took quite a while for expansion to spread out that heat. But eventually, more and more electrons were able to latch on to atomic nuclei and form neutral atoms, which are much more transparent than individual electrons. Around 300,000 years after the Big Bang, the dense, hot fog of matter in the Universe was suddenly transparent enough to set the energetic photons free to travel long, long distances.

Ralph Alpher and Robert Herman were students of George Gamow in 1948. They calculated that the incredibly hot photons from that early time must still be zipping across the Universe today. Also, the photons should radiate smoothly from all directions, since the early Universe was filled with them. As the Universe continued to expand, this radiation cooled off. Alpher and Herman were able to calculate how cold this primal radiation should be by now.

It was in 1965 that the background radiation was actually observed. Two radio engineers in New Jersey, Arno Penzias and Robert Wilson, noticed a noisy static whenever they tested their microwave radio receiver by aiming it at the sky. Now called the "cosmic background," this was the actual radiation from the photons that were released 300,000 years after the Big Bang! It is one of the most important proofs that the Big Bang really happened. For their discovery, Penzias and Wilson were awarded the Nobel Prize.

An orbiting satellite was launched in 1989 specifically to look closely at the photons from the early Universe. Called the *Cosmic Background Explorer*, or

COBE, it verified that the radiation left over from the Big Bang is coming almost equally from all directions of the background sky and that the current temperature of the Universe is -454.8°F (-270.5°C). It could even be said that the Big Bang is not over yet—though it is much calmer today.

Early in 2003, an orbital spacecraft called the *Wilkinson Microwave Anisotropy Probe* (WMAP) also surveyed the Universe for fluctuations in the cosmic background. And the data it collected was used to create a photographic image. The details are in sharper focus than any previous image of the photons left over after the Big Bang. Using the data, scientists calculated that the Universe is 13.7×10^9 (13.7 billion) years old—which agrees with Wendy Freedman's approximate value. The tiny dark blotches in the picture show where galaxies eventually formed. WMAP was named after David Wilkinson, a cosmology expert from Princeton University, who passed away in 2002.

Illustration of the **COBE** spacecraft, which confirmed that radiation from the Big Bang permeates the Universe. **Notice the solar panels extending from either side, which turn sunlight into electricity to power the craft.**

The Birth of Galaxies

CHAPTER FIVE

Galaxies are communities of billions of stars. They are the grandest sights in the Universe. There is great variety in their appearance and their beauty. Some are tilted so that their spiral structure is plain to see; others are seen edge-on (as though we were looking down on them from above), with distinctive bulges in their middles. The Milky Way is our home galaxy, and it's about 100,000 light-years across—which is about average in size.

Closer inspection shows that, inside the swirling arms of galaxies, there are glowing blobs and delicate dark filaments. Big telescopes can even pinpoint individual stars in many galaxies. But the view can also be pulled back to reveal a wider field. Astronomer Charles Messier, in the 18th century, noticed that there were a lot of fuzzy patches gathered together in a part of the constellation Virgo. This was the first discovery of a "cluster" of galaxies. Galaxy clusters are now known to group dozens or even thousands of individual galaxies together.

How did these wondrous baubles get hung in the sky like this? The Universe cooked them up somehow. If all of space were as smooth as the creamiest of puddings, there'd be no galaxies and no galaxy clusters. Seeing them is proof that clumps of matter got stuck together at some point in the history of the Universe.

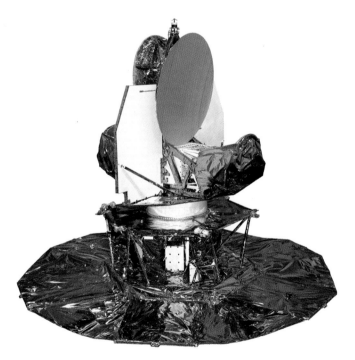

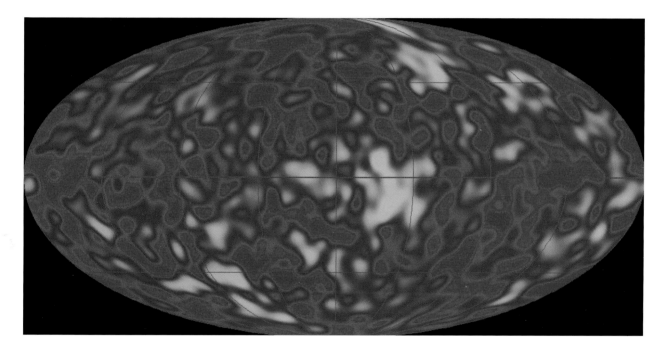

There were tiny, random concentrations of matter at the beginning of the Inflationary Period. They resulted from all the bumping and jostling of the incredibly high-energy nuclear particles and waves that existed then instead of ordinary matter. While the Universe was growing so dramatically from 10^{-35} to 10^{-33} seconds, the uneven fluctuations grew with it, and they remained after the Inflationary Period ended.

This made up the graininess of the early Universe. These ripples of unevenness were first measured by the COBE satellite between 1989 and 1993. Other experiments to measure the graininess of the early Universe have been flown on

A map of the Universe generated by data acquired by the COBE spacecraft. The darker (red) spots show areas in the Universe where matter lumped together in the just-born Universe. This unequal distribution of matter gave rise to the stars and galaxies.

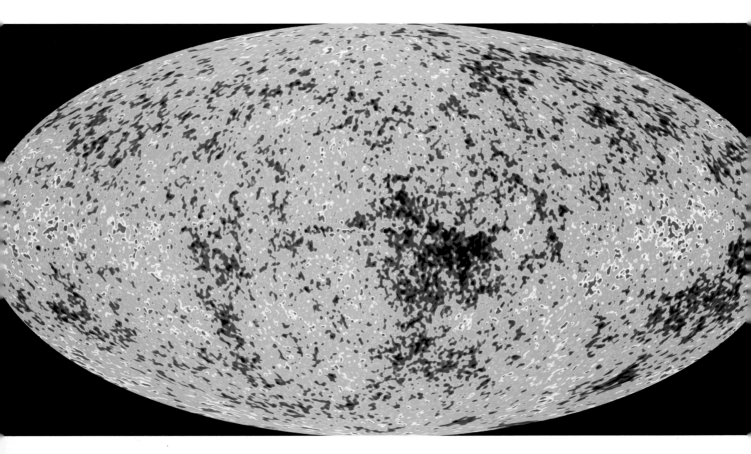

The WMAP spacecraft surveyed the Universe looking for the temperatures generated by the background radiation of the Big Bang. Areas where matter was denser were warmer than other areas. The darker spots (blue) show where matter originally clumped after the Big Bang. These are the places where galaxies first formed.

large balloons, such as the BOOMERANG project in Antarctica. And the most precise view of the lumpiness of the early Universe comes from the WMAP spacecraft. All of this is part of the continuing effort to understand and explain how galaxies and galaxy clusters could have developed in a Universe that was thought to have been born completely smooth. Cosmologists had assumed that the Big Bang created the building blocks of matter and spewed them forth into the expanding Universe at the same rate in all directions, with the same quality of smoothness. Scientists now know that the Universe was born with lumps.

As space continued to expand and cool somewhat, gravity pulled the fluctuations together, concentrating them. On a cosmic scale, gravity doesn't act quickly.

But it is persistent, and there was no hurry. When the fog of the Big Bang finally cleared and radiation was set free, the only clumps that were left over were big enough to harbor the matter for entire galaxies and clusters of galaxies. Scientists also think "black holes" formed alongside most of the infant galaxies. A black hole is a spot in space where gravity has collapsed in on itself, and neither matter nor energy can get out. Recent evidence hints that black holes "swallowed" as much as 20 percent of the original matter that was available to form into galaxies.

Scientists are not sure what happened next to the young galaxies. Did the galaxy clusters form first, and then break apart to form individual galaxies? Or did galaxies condense one by one—smaller ones first, larger galaxies later—and then gather together to form the giant clusters? Either way, the Universe ended up with vast wisps and knots of galaxies, spread through all of space and separated by even more vast zones of emptiness. Think of a cosmic foam, mostly empty and gradually spreading out. Galaxies formed along the surfaces where the bubbles of foam would contact each other, with the empty insides of the bubbles representing the voids between the cascades of galaxies—the empty spaces of outer space.

Wherever astronomers look, they see galaxies almost beyond numbering. (The total number of galaxies in the Universe today is estimated at more than 100 billion.) The *Hubble Space Telescope* took two famous pictures by peering as deep into intergalactic space as possible. These were called the "Hubble Deep Field" pictures, one in the northern half of the sky and the other in the southern half. There are *thousands* of galaxies in each picture.

An artist's concept of a black hole at the center of a galaxy. The black hole draws in energy, matter, and light. But some subatomic particles are so energized by the process that they stream out north and south of the black hole, causing streaks of energy that can be seen through optical telescopes.

Image shot by the *Hubble Space Telescope* of the most distant galaxies in the Universe. Each image here is a galaxy. The oldest date back almost 13 billion years, which is probably when the very first galaxies were forming.

The appearance of the farthest galaxies is typical of the way all galaxies looked many billions of years ago, about a billion years after the Big Bang. There are a lot of faint blue dwarf galaxies in the deepest pictures. It's possible that most galaxies were like that when they first formed. Based on analysis of thousands of galaxies in the Hubble Deep Field pictures, astronomers speculate that there was an intense time of star formation in the first few million years after the Big Bang. In the eons that have passed since then, the basic shape of galaxies has changed a little because they have been spinning. Just like Earth and our entire solar system, each galaxy rotates around a central point. That's why so many have that beautiful, characteristic spiral form.

Sequence from the Big Bang to the creation of galaxies. The Inflationary Period saw the greatest expansion of the Universe, which, after a few hundred thousand years, already had clumps of matter that would eventually form into stars and galaxies.

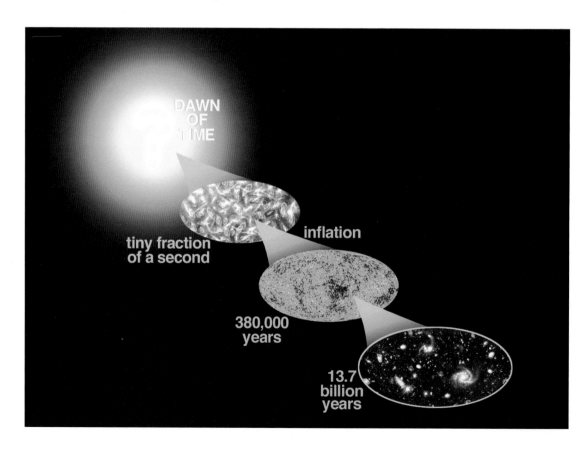

DAWN OF TIME

tiny fraction of a second

inflation

380,000 years

13.7 billion years

The Mystery of What We Can't See

All across the Universe, galaxies are doing majestic turns. The Milky Way is estimated to be almost 13 billion years old—not much less than the age of the Universe. It takes more than 100 million years for the stars in a typical spiral arm to revolve all the way around their home galaxy. Even though this is only a fraction of the age of the Universe, it is still a very long time. In the Milky Way, the speeds of thousands of individual stars and interstellar gas clouds have been measured. Since the time it first formed out of such a cloud of gases, our Sun has made about 19 complete circuits around our galaxy.

Closer investigation revealed that the stars and clouds closer to the center of the Milky Way move faster, and those farther from the center move less quickly. Our solar system, located on a spiral arm about 30,000 light-years from the center of the Milky Way, is being passed by others on what would be the "inside tracks."

The only reason why the rotation of the galaxy is more complicated than satellites in orbit around Earth is that the mass of the galaxy is spread out, with more of it in the bright, central bulge and less and less mass farther out. Measurements of the direction and speed of all the motions give a detailed picture of exactly how much mass is in the middle of the galaxy compared with the outer regions.

Fritz Zwicky, who worked at the Palomar Observatory in California in the middle of the 20th century, was first to realize that there was a conflict between the observable mass of the galaxy and the rate of its rotation. He compared what was known about the number of visible stars and gas clouds in the Milky Way Galaxy with the mass obtained from studying their motions, and the two figures didn't match. The objects farther away from the center of the galaxy were expected to be traveling more slowly. Indeed, they were moving more slowly—but not

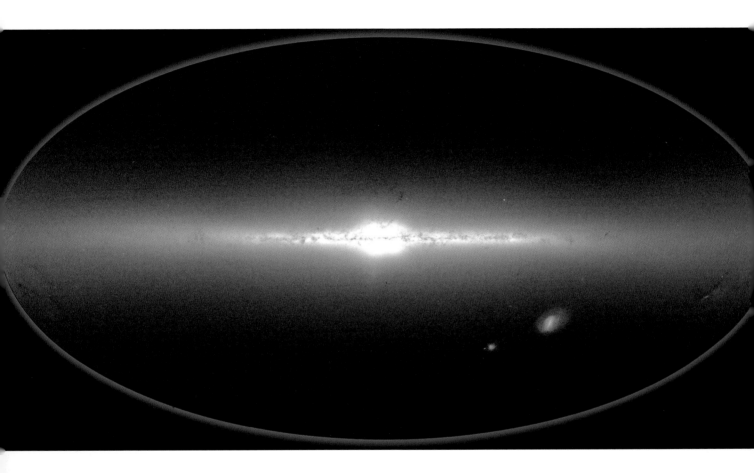

An optical image pieced together from a telescopic survey of the sky shows the Milky Way Galaxy seen edge on. Note the Large and Small Magellanic Clouds below and to the right of the galaxy. They are satellites of the Milky Way and our nearest galactic neighbors.

as slowly as predicted. The calculations showed that there was 10 times as much mass in the Milky Way Galaxy as can be seen by looking at the night sky. The farther out from the middle of the Milky Way that astronomers looked, the more of a difference they saw between the visible matter and the mass that causes the gravity. The force of gravity in the spiral arms is 50 times stronger than can be explained by the stars, gas clouds, and star clusters that we can see, even allowing for a lot of dim stars and cold gas. This means that most of the mass in our galaxy is unseen and has not yet been discovered.

Other galaxies, millions of light-years away, show the same effect. James Peebles and Vera Rubin are among the researchers who have made such measurements. The results are clear: every galaxy has a greater gravity than can be explained by its visible matter. On an even larger scale, astronomers have measured the speed of individual members in clusters of galaxies. There, too, the measured speeds do not fit. Clearly, galaxies contain a lot more matter than just the objects in them that we can see. All in all, the estimate of how much invisible matter is contained in galaxy clusters is *100 times more* than the visible matter. Astronomers have named this mysterious stuff "dark matter." It is so mysterious that scientists don't yet know what it is made of.

Einstein's theory of relativity has also been applied to this puzzle. Since space is curved around heavy objects, an entire galaxy bends light rays that pass by it. The light rays will bend more if the galaxy contains more mass. The bending of light rays by galaxies has been measured. And this, too, has provided solid evidence that the invisible matter really is out there.

Ideas abound concerning the nature of the dark matter. It can't be anti-matter, or it would have annihilated the ordinary matter in the Universe long ago. Could it be a whole

This spiral galaxy shows how visible matter thins out toward the edges of the spiral arms. But unseen "dark matter" holds it together.

population of miniature black holes? What about planet-sized objects roaming freely around the fringe of the galaxy? Perhaps it is exotic atomic particles, such as neutrinos, magnetic monopoles, or strange new particles that have never been observed in our laboratories.

How is the dark matter spread throughout the Universe? It would be natural to assume that most of the dark matter would be found in the dark voids *between* the largest clusters of galaxies. This interesting question was answered in 2002 by the unfinished galaxy maps of the 2dF Galaxy Redshift Survey. They clearly show the galaxies strung out across space like glittering necklaces. Using this data, the scientists were also able to figure out where the dark matter is. The conclusion is that there is not a significant amount of dark matter in the great cosmic voids. Most of it resides *within* the galaxies. This means that whatever the dark matter might turn out to be, it probably formed alongside ordinary matter in the tiny ripples of the Big Bang.

Four galaxies are being ripped apart by strong gravitational forces. They are so close that the four take up the same total amount of volume in space as the Milky Way does. The fact that these galaxies are so close to each other is a result of the clumps of matter in the early Universe being unevenly distributed. (A fifth galaxy, seen top-down, is much farther away from the grouping and is not affected by the gravitational pull of the other four galaxies.)

Some 300 million light-years from Earth, these two galaxies, dubbed "the Mice" because of their long gaseous tails, are colliding. Local gravity—including that generated by dark matter—is strong enough so that these two galaxies will eventually merge into one larger galaxy.

The 2dF Galaxy Redshift Survey

An exciting research project that is looking at a huge chunk of the Universe is the 2dF Galaxy Redshift Survey. "2dF" stands for "two degree field," which is a measurement of how much of the sky is shown on each picture taken. 2dF uses the 150-inch (3.9 m) Anglo-Australian Telescope, which is located near Coonabarabran in Australia. The 2dF camera works by aiming 400 fiber-optic cables at individual galaxies through the telescope. Then the colors from each of the 400 galaxies are recorded, their redshifts are calculated, and the computer software adds them to the diagram of the whole Universe. Starting in 1999, the mission goal of the 2dF scientists has been to capture 250,000 separate galaxies in a wide region of the sky. There is an even more ambitious project underway in the northern hemisphere called the Sloan Digital Sky Survey.

Where Are the Galaxies Going?

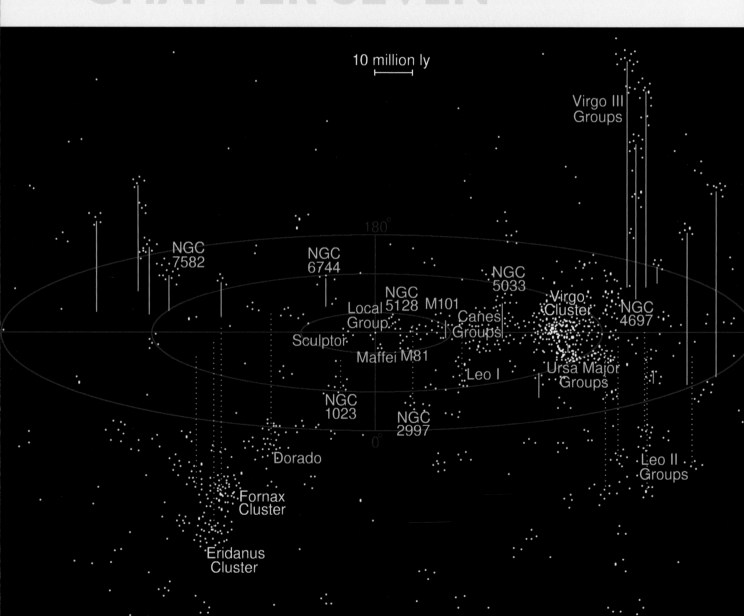

CHAPTER SEVEN

10 million ly

Virgo III
Groups

180°

NGC
7582

NGC
6744

NGC
5128

NGC
5033

Local
Group

M101

Virgo
Cluster

NGC
4697

Sculptor

Canes
Groups

Maffei M81

Leo I

Ursa Major
Groups

0°

NGC
1023

NGC
2997

Leo II
Groups

Dorado

Fornax
Cluster

Eridanus
Cluster

Even sitting in a chair, a person moves quite fast through the Universe. Not only are we all spinning with Earth and orbiting the Sun, but the Sun is also traveling around our Milky Way Galaxy. And that's not the end of it, either: the entire Milky Way is rushing headlong through space, more or less in the direction of the Andromeda Galaxy, our nearest galactic neighbor.

Beginning in the 1930s, Clyde Tombaugh, George Abell, and other astronomers became convinced that the galaxies in the Universe, enormous as they are, group together in clusters. Even the clusters seem to be gathered into clusters of clusters, called "superclusters." The Milky Way Galaxy, the Andromeda Galaxy, the Pinwheel Galaxy in the constellation Triangulum, and 14 other galaxies, all within a few million light-years of each other, are known as "the Local Group." And they all belong to the Virgo Supercluster. This is Earth's home system. Farther out, but still within less than one-tenth of the distance across the Universe, there are 80 superclusters, and they contain something like 3 million galaxies similar to the Milky Way. Smaller galaxies in these superclusters number about 10 times that.

The whole Virgo Supercluster is also moving together as a giant family among all the other superclusters. Alan Dressler and six other scientists discovered that the speed of this motion is about 250 miles (400 km) per second. Our destination on this celestial ride is an enormous supercluster in the direction of the constellation

The all-sky surveys have provided us with maps that note the distribution of local and distant galaxies. Mapping all of the galaxies within about 75 light-years, we can see that they tend to be unevenly distributed, forming clumps in some places and leaving great voids in others. Our Milky Way is part of the Virgo cluster.

Centaurus. The Milky Way Galaxy is out near the fringe of this larger supercluster, but the center is at least 150 million light-years away. Even the incredible speed at which the Virgo Supercluster is moving does not bring us much closer to Centaurus in the span of our lifetimes.

Something extremely massive must be pulling the Virgo Supercluster toward Centaurus. It is probably the gravity of another supercluster located beyond Centaurus—a supercluster that has 10^{15} stars and a lot of hidden dark matter. Dressler called this colossal source of gravity the "Great Attractor." Unfortunately, our view in that direction is partly obscured by matter in the outer reaches of the Milky Way itself. This makes it difficult for astronomers to get reliable data about what's going on closer to the center of the Great Attractor.

Taking a final, huge step back to look at the motions of all the galaxies in the Universe, we would see them roaring apart because of the expansion that started in the Big Bang. In 1998, astronomers discovered that the expansion of the Universe is speeding up. By measuring supernovas in some very distant galaxies, researchers saw that galaxies had moved more slowly long ago and are moving somewhat faster today. The way things are going, the Universe will thin out, and eventually the galaxies will not even be able to see each other. This will take another 40 billion years or so.

The fact that the Universe is not just expanding but expanding *at an increasing rate* took scientists by surprise. Previously, astronomers thought that the gravity from all the matter in the Universe—especially the recently discovered dark matter—was strong enough to either stop the expansion eventually, or at least slow it down enough so that the Universe would approach some maximum size.

Here is a map of all of the galaxies within 750 million light-years of Earth. Patterns of denseness and emptiness are clearly seen. The gravity generated by visible and dark matter causes the galaxies to group together. But mysterious dark energy is pushing all matter in the Universe out and away in an unending expansion.

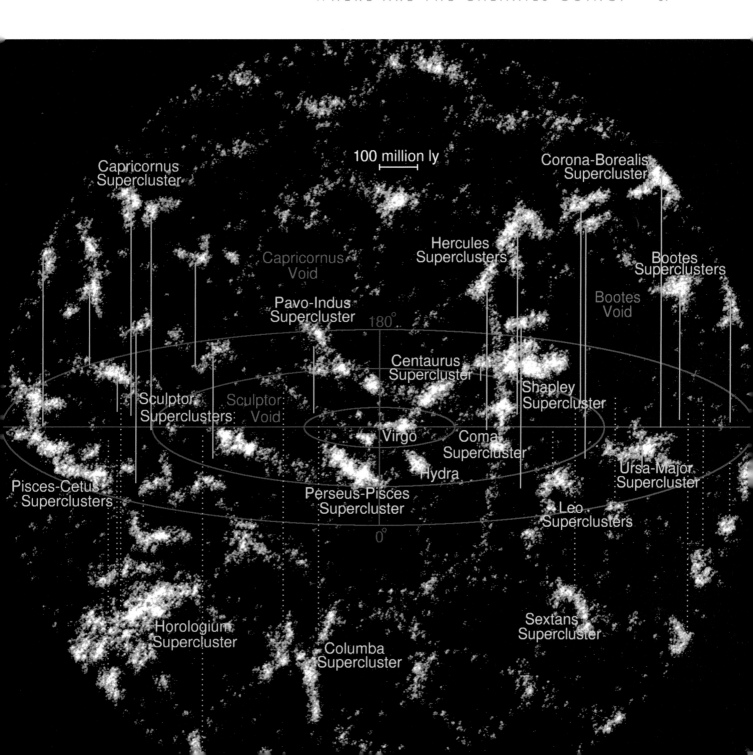

Capricornus
Supercluster

100 million ly

Corona-Borealis
Supercluster

Capricornus
Void

Hercules
Superclusters

Bootes
Superclusters

Bootes
Void

Pavo-Indus
Supercluster

180°

Centaurus
Supercluster

Shapley
Supercluster

Sculptor
Superclusters

Sculptor
Void

Virgo

Coma
Supercluster

Ursa-Major
Supercluster

Pisces-Cetus
Superclusters

Hydra

Perseus-Pisces
Supercluster

Leo
Superclusters

0°

Horologium
Supercluster

Sextans
Supercluster

Columba
Supercluster

Because the expansion started with the Big Bang, astronomers had thought the galaxies were coasting outward, gliding along without needing a push. But galaxies are speeding up, and so there must be a *continuing* push.

Where could this push come from? The answer is still being discussed by experts. It cannot be gravity, because gravity can only pull something toward something else. What could repel an object the size of an entire galaxy? None of the four forces that scientists understand well could do that. Astronomers are concentrating on the possibility that a fifth force exists, one that has no effect on people or even on the whole Earth. It would be a force that works only across huge distances in space. Some scientists have already suggested that it be named "quintessence," after the heavenly, fifth form of matter from ancient Greek cosmology.

But this quintessence, if it exists, is not material. Rather, it is a form of energy. Other scientists have started calling it "dark energy." Like dark matter, it is invisible, except for its effect on the speed of galaxies. It is even possible to make some preliminary calculations about how much dark energy there would have to be to make the galaxies speed up the way they do. The answer is truly stupendous: the amount would have to be twice as much as all the other forms of energy and matter in the Universe.

The final picture as it develops indicates a Universe that is mostly dark energy, with dark matter the second most important part. Normal matter and normal energy, as we know them, are but a tiny fraction of everything.

Some of the unseen matter in the Universe is in the form of black holes. (Black holes are invisible but extremely energetic, and Einstein proved that energy and matter are equivalent.) In this illustration, a robotic probe takes measurements of a massive black hole that is in the process of eating up the matter that surrounds it, including any nearby planets and stars.

The Universe as a Ball of String?

CHAPTER EIGHT

It is a wild and whimsical idea, but mathematicians are taking it seriously: What if everything in the Universe is made of bits of primordial string? The "string" that cosmologists are studying these days, however, is not the kind that keeps a kite connected to its flyer. There are some weird things going on with so-called "cosmological string."

The regular space that we live in has three well-known dimensions called length, width, and height. It's common to consider time to be the fourth dimension, and that already makes the equations of physics quite complicated. In string theory, extra dimensions are called for. With 10 dimensions, mathematicians think they can explain most of what goes on in the Universe.

To understand what this means, we need to begin by imagining not extra dimensions, but *fewer*. A sheet of paper, for instance, has only two dimensions. Draw a shape—any shape—made of dots joined by straight lines. Now roll the paper up—which requires that you turn the sheet in the third dimension—and then look only at the end of the roll. All you see in this end-on view is a circle. If the paper were transparent, you could see the dots and lines at different positions around the circle. While the real figure you drew is still there in the original two dimensions, those dimensions are wrapped up into the circle. To understand "reality," you would have to analyze what you see, account for the curvature of the visible circle, and figure out what the original figure looked like.

In the 1920s, Oskar Klein and Theodor Kaluza studied the idea of adding extra dimensions to some famous theories of physics. They interpreted the world we see as a three- or four-dimensional "end view" of 10 dimensions—or perhaps even more—of reality. Although no one can visualize what a 10-dimensional

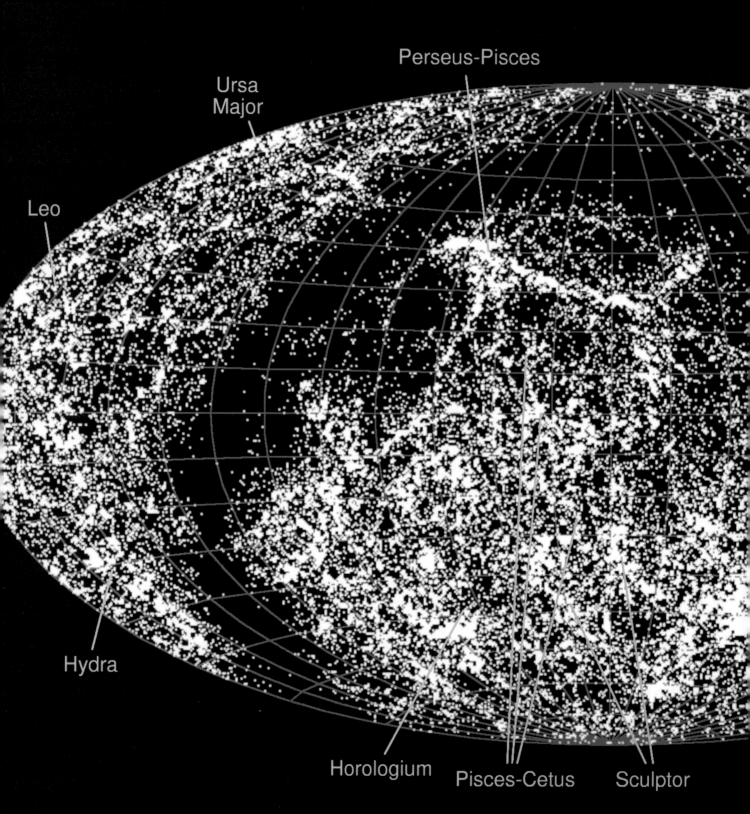

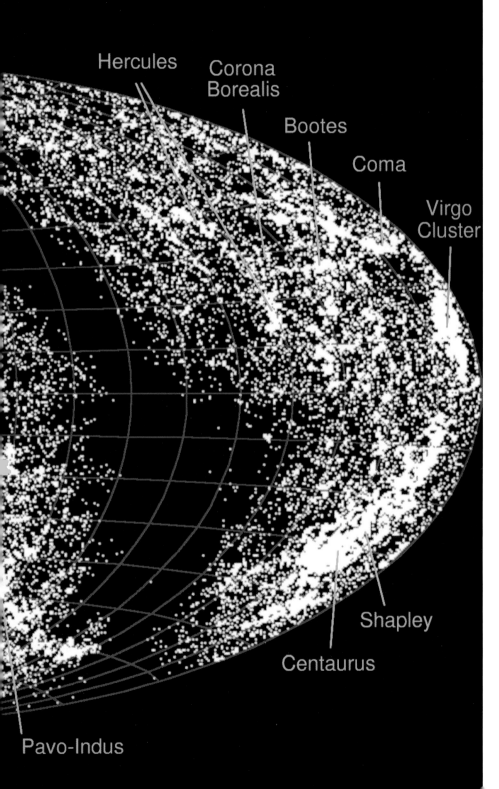

Hercules

Corona
Borealis

Bootes

Coma

Virgo
Cluster

Shapley

Centaurus

Pavo-Indus

This sky-survey map shows the 60,000 brightest galaxies, as seen from Earth. Now the vast collections of galaxies are grouped into sheets and wall-like structures. And the empty spaces are stark in comparison. Still, visible matter—stars, planets, galaxies, and nebulae—accounts for only five percent of the Universe. Dark matter and dark energy may account for the rest. Or perhaps string theory can provide the answer to the question of where the "missing matter" is.

world would look like, mathematics experts can write down the appropriate equations. Eventually, mathematicians worked out a scheme that explains six of these dimensions as being "wrapped-up" in string-like shapes that are less than 10^{-35} meters in size! The scale is so incredibly tiny that even the extreme conditions of the Primordial Atom would not unwrap them. According to this theory, in the Big Bang *all* the dimensions start out compacted this way. The four dimensions we know then unraveled themselves as the Big Bang proceeded, while the others would have remained forever hidden. This is the basis of what the experts now call "string theory."

On the very small scale of string theory, reality should show evidence of remarkable symmetry. That means someone could look at a scene from different points of view and still see the same thing. In the example of the two-dimensional drawing on paper, viewing the rolled-up paper from the other end would still make it look like a circle. If string theory is an accurate way of describing the Universe, then something similar is happening in the real world. All the subatomic particles that scientists have learned about would have symmetrical twins. The balance between the symmetrical particles would be not quite perfect. This description seems appropriate for the conditions at the time of the Big Bang. The challenge is to come up with ways to test string theories in the laboratory. None of the extra symmetrical particles have yet been discovered, because no laboratory has a machine powerful enough to observe any of these particles. However, some scientists think that symmetrical particles might be part of the dark matter of the Universe.

Another inspiring possibility is that the symmetry of the extra dimensions might have split off *independent* three- or four-dimensional universes, like blowing soap bubbles, in the earliest moments of the Big Bang. These other universes might still be out there, even though no interaction with our own is possible.

In the coming years, mathematicians may learn to apply string theory to cosmology and predict what astronomers will find as they study the data from the farthest reaches of the Universe. If astronomers verify that the calculations of string theory correctly describe what is seen, then scientists will have answered the questions of what our Universe is made of, where it came from, and what might happen to it long after they're gone. Such a theory has already been given a name by researchers—they call it "the Theory of Everything." And to think it might be all wrapped in an imaginary ball of string!

The Moebius Strip

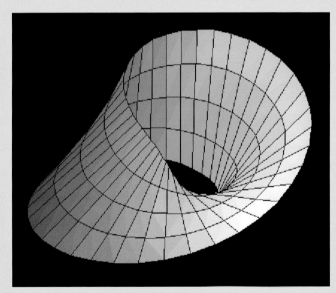

An illustration of a Moebius Strip, which has but a single surface.

August Moebius was a mathematics professor at the University of Leipzig in the 19th century. He designed a simple construction now called a Moebius Strip. The Moebius Strip is one of the simplest shapes in the branch of mathematics called topology. And topology is the basis for string theory. Here's how to construct one.

1. Take a piece of paper or ribbon an inch (a few cm) wide and about eight inches (20 cm) long.

2. Bring one end around to the other like you are about to buckle a belt.

3. Give one end a half twist, and then join the two ends together with tape or glue.

4. The result is a shape that has only one side, instead of an inside and an outside.

5. Prove this by taking a pen or a marker and drawing a long line down the middle of the Moebius Strip.

Notice that, when your line finally joins back up with itself, it has covered the entire Moebius Strip. There is no second side left unmarked.

G L O S S A R Y

anti-quark A basic particle of matter that carries a fractional electric charge.

atomic nuclei Central portion of atoms that comprise almost all the atomic mass and consist of protons and neutrons.

black hole A place in space where gravity has collapsed in on itself and neither matter nor energy can escape.

blue shift A change in the color spectrum of a celestial object as the object moves toward an observer.

cosmic background Static emanating from the Universe; radiation coming from photons from the initial expansion of the Universe.

cosmology Branch of science that deals with the Universe as an orderly system.

dark energy Invisible form of energy that is the opposite of gravity and is theorized to be the fifth basic force.

Doppler shift Change in frequency of sound, light, or radio waves as they approach and then go past an observer.

electromagnetism The attraction or repulsion of charged particles. One of the four basic forces of nature.

electron Basic atomic particle having a negative electric charge.

galaxy A system that includes stars, nebulae, star clusters, globular clusters, and interstellar matter. Approximately 100 billion of these systems exist in the Universe.

globular clusters Sphere-shaped groups of thousands of stars, usually associated with galaxies.

Grand Unification Name given to theory about the combining of three of the basic forces of nature: electromagnetism, weak nuclear force, and strong nuclear force.

gravity The force that attracts masses to each other. One of the four basic forces of nature.

Great Attractor A colossal source of gravity; probably a massive supercluster of galaxies.

Inflationary Period Occurring shortly after the Big Bang, a brief period when outward expansion of the Universe was even faster than at the beginning.

light-year Unit of length in astronomy equal to distance light travels in one year in a vacuum; approximately six trillion miles (10 trillion km).

Local Group Cluster of galaxies that includes our galaxy, the Milky Way, as well as Andromeda, Pinwheel, and 14 other galaxies.

Milky Way Galaxy The system that contains the solar system as well as countless stars, nebulae, star clusters, globular clusters, and interstellar matter; our galaxy.

Moebius Strip A construction that results in a shape having only one side.

nebulae Immense bodies of gas and/or dust in interstellar space.

photon A particle of energy that can act as a carrier wave; light propagates through protons.

positron Basic particle having a positive electric charge. The anti-matter twin of an electron, it is also called a positive electron.

quark One of the basic particles of matter, it has a fractional electric charge.

quasar Quasi-stellar radio source.

quintessence The fifth form of matter proposed by Greek philosophers. It existed only in space, according to ancient thinkers.

red shift A change in the color spectrum of a celestial object as it moves away from an observer.

scientific notation System used by scientists and cosmologists who deal with extremely large numbers in their calculations. It is based on the decimal number system and powers of 10.

spectroscope Instrument used to observe the colors of light spread out in a spectrum, that is, in the same order as a rainbow.

string theory Theory about unseen dimensions in string-like shapes thought necessary by scientists and mathematicians to explain the Universe. It proposes 10 dimensions for the Universe.

strong nuclear force Attraction of quarks to each other. One of the four basic forces of nature, it is very powerful inside an atomic nucleus.

supernova The explosive end to a giant star's existence.

topology Branch of mathematics concerned with properties of geometric configurations (point sets) which are not altered by elastic deformations, like twisting and stretching.

Virgo Supercluster The enormous group of clustered galaxies of which we are part.

weak nuclear force Attraction of nuclear particles, basically protons and neutrons, in the nuclei of atoms. One of the four basic forces of nature, it applies only among nuclear particles.

Abell, George, 37
Air, 7
Alpher, Ralph, 22
Ancient Greece, 7, 40
Andromeda (galaxy), 9
   organization of, 37
Anti-matter, 21
Anti-quarks, 21
Atom, 10, 22

B
Balloons, 26
Big Bang, 18
   dimensions, creation of, 44
   Grand Unification, 20
   Inflationary Period, 21
   matter, creation of, 26
   proof of, 22
   radiation, direction of, 23
Black hole, 27
Blue shift, 11
BOOMERANG project
   (Antarctica), 26

C
Centaurus (constellation), 38
China, 8
Cluster (galactic), 24
   grouping of, 37
COBE (Cosmic Background
   Explorer), 23, 25
Coonabarabran (Australia),
   35
Cosmic background, 22
   exploration of, 25
   fluctuations in, 23
Creation myths, 7, 10

D
Dark Ages, 8
Dark matter, 33, 38
Definitions
   black hole, 27
   cosmology, 7
   globular cluster, 14
   light-year, 9
   nebulae, 9
   primeval, 15
Dimensions (spatial), 41
   Universe, shape of, 12
Doppler shift, 11
Dressler, Alan, 37
Dwarf galaxies, 30

E
Earth (element), 7
Earth (planet)
   age of, 9
   home system of, 37
   rotation of, 30
Einstein, Albert, 12, 15
Electromagnetism, 19
Electrons, 21
Energy, 18
   Big Bang, generated by, 22
   black hole, 27
   galaxies, speed of, 40
Eudoxus, 7
Europe
   astronomy, development
     of, 9
   Dark Ages, 8
Expansion
   acceleration of, 38
   discovery of, 10
   evidence as to, 13

Inflationary Period, 21
   shape, effect on, 12
Exponent (mathematics), 6

F
Fire, 7
Fluctuations, 23, 26
Freedman, Wendy, 12

G
Galaxies, 5
   appearance of, 30
   creation of, 25
   dark matter in, 33
   described, 24
   development of, 26
   distance measurement, 9
   dwarf galaxies, 30
   expansion, acceleration
     of, 38
   Hubble's Law, 12
   Milky Way. See Milky Way
   movement, discovery of,
     10
   number of, 27
   rotation period, 31
Galilei, Galileo, 9
Gamow, George, 18
Gas clouds, 31
Geology, 9
Globular cluster, 14
Grand Unification, 20
Gravity, 19
   black hole, creation of, 27
   matter, creation of, 26
   Milky Way, 32
   Virgo, effect on, 38
Great Attractor
   (supercluster), 38

Guth, Alan, 21

H
Herman, Robert, 22
Hertzprung-Russell diagram,
   14
Hoyle, Fred, 18
Hubble, Edwin, 10
   discovery of, 12
Hubble Space Telescope, 13, 27

I
Inflationary Period, 21

K
Kaluza, Theodor, 41
Kelvin, Lord William
   Thomson, 9
Klein, Oskar, 41

L
Lemaitre, George Edouard,
   15
Light wave, 11
   relativity theory, 15
Light-year, 9
   Milky Way Galaxy, 24
   stars, age of, 14
Local Group, 37
Lowell Observatory, Arizona,
   10

M
Mass (physics), 15
Mathematics, 6, 44
Matter, 18, 21
   birth of, 25
   black holes, role of, 27

Greek philosophy, 7
invisible matter, estimates
of, 33
Messier, Charles, 24
Milky Way
age of, 31
globular clusters, 14
mass of, 32
organization of, 37
Moebius, August, 45
Moebius Strip, 45

N
Natural forces, 19
Big Bang, effect of, 20
discovery involving, 40
Primeval Atom, conditions
in, 18
Nebulae, 9
Neutrinos, 34

O
Orbit, 9

P
Palomar Observatory (CA),
31
Particle accelerator, 5
Peebles, James, 33
Penzias, Arno, 22
Period
matter, birth of, 25
Photon, 22

Physics, 11
Pinwheel (galaxy), 37
Positron, 21
Primeval Atom, 15
conditions in, 18
string theory, 44

Q
Quarks, 21
Quasar, 5
Quintessence, 7, 40

R
Radiation, 22, 23
Radioactivity, 9
Red shift, 11
2dF Galaxy Redshift
Survey, 35
Relativity theory, 12
discoveries based on, 15
invisible matter, 33
Rotation, 31, 37
Rubin, Vera, 33
Rutherford, Sir Ernest, 9

S
Satellites (artificial), 23
Scientific notation, 6
Big Bang, 20
Singularity, 18
Slipher, Vesto, 10
Sloan Digital Sky Survey, 35
Solar eclipse, 15

Solar system, 9, 31
Space, 13, 15, 27
Spectroscope, 11
Speed, 37
Doppler shift, 11
galaxy, 12
Stars, 24
age of, 14
formation of, 30
String theory, 41
basis of, 44
Strong nuclear force, 19
Subatomic particles, 44
Sun (star), 9
orbit of, 37
rotation period, 31
warping effect, 15
Supercluster (galactic), 37
Supernova, 9, 38
Symmetrical particles, 44

T
Telescope
Anglo-Australian tele-
scope, 35
Hubble Deep Field
pictures, 27, 30
invention of, 9
radio telescope, 22
Temperature, 23
Thales, 7
Theory of Everything, 45
Time, 15, 20

Tombaugh, Clyde, 37
Topology, 45
Triangulum (constellation), 37

U
Universe
age of, 6, 13
Big Bang theory. See Big
Bang
birth of, 15
composition of, 9
expansion of, 10, 38
graininess of, 25
shape of, 12
size of, 5
string theory, 41
V
Virgo (supercluster)
creation of, 24
gravity, effect of, 38
speed and direction of, 37

W
Water
Ancient Greek philosophy
on, 7
Weak nuclear force, 19
Wilkinson, David, 23
Wilson, Robert, 22
WMAP (space probe), 23, 26

Z
Zwicky, Fritz, 31